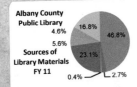

BEYOND BULLETS

A PHOTO JOURNAL OF AFGHANISTAN

BY RAFAL GERSZAK
WITH DAWN HUNTER

annick press
toronto + new york + vancouver

FOREWORD

"Ding!" It looks like such an inoffensive word. Four letters, one syllable, impossible to speak without a sing-song tone, an inflection point for a child's story. Amazing how our words capture so little of what happens in Afghanistan. "Ding" hardly describes the sound of a bullet fired from a Kalashnikov rifle narrowly missing you, striking metal with a high note so pure that it would seem musical in another context. "Ding! ding! ding! ding!" A terrifying succession of notes. Those are the words Rafal Gerszak uses to describe the sound of gunfire raking his vehicle during an ambush. For me, his writing evokes all the intensity of battle, because we have shared many of the same experiences. I've also listened to the ping of bullets off armour near my head, also heard a bullet smack a thick window in front of my nose, also leapt out of bed after the impact of a rocket nearby. Like him, too, I sense that language fails when we talk about war. We cannot tell you about the full experience, because nothing quite says it. "The smells, the sounds, the chaos—it's impossible to describe," he writes, and unfortunately he is correct. I've just finished writing a book of my own, about travels in Afghanistan from 2005 to 2009, and often felt despair at the inadequacy of my words.

Photography has always been a better medium for documenting war, and Rafal's powerful images convey things that do not fit comfortably into a paragraph. The man painting a white bird onto the raw concrete bulk of a blast wall reminds me of all the times Afghans eked a little beauty out of their harsh surroundings: the rifles decorated with fake flowers, the trucks painted with garden scenes as they rumbled through empty desert. You do not need to feel the dry furnace of Afghan summer to appreciate how a boy yearns for water in the moment before he dives into a pool. You don't need a writer like me to tell you the story of a woman's survival—her suffering, her escapes—when you see the decades of worry on her face. Many other photographers have aimed their cameras at identical scenes; I've taken thousands of my own snapshots in similar places, but somehow none of my images show Afghanistan's magic. I'm not sure how he did it, but Rafal manages to distill some of that essence with his lens. His photos reveal a country in motion, off-balance, always reeling in aftermath or tense with anticipation of the next incident. My friends and relatives ask me what it's like in Afghanistan, and my summary is the same as Rafal's: "It's a mess." How can I elaborate? Maybe next time, I'll pull out a copy of this book and show them his photographs. They spell out the awful situation, with grace and simplicity.

Graeme Smith
The Globe and Mail
Istanbul, Feb. 2011

I am a photojournalist who has worked with news agencies, media outlets, magazines, newspapers, websites, and galleries. For a long time I specialized in covering various topics at home through my photography. Then, in 2008, I moved to Afghanistan. At first, I tried to go to Afghanistan with the Canadian military—journalists can be embedded with a military unit, which means we live and travel with them. I was put on a waiting list and told it would take more than a year.

I got frustrated with waiting, so I looked for another way in. I'm Polish, so I thought about embedding with Polish troops, which at that time were under American command. I got in touch with the U.S. Army public affairs officer for Afghanistan. He sent me my paperwork, I applied, and three weeks later I received my approval letter.

Getting to Afghanistan, it turns out, was the easy part. The hard part was getting to the front lines. After weeks of being trapped on Bagram Air Base and Forward Operating Base Salerno, and hitting dead end after dead end, I went to the public affairs office again and begged them to get me out to where the combat operations were taking place. I couldn't take any more pictures of guys playing volleyball and barbecuing.

My persistence worked. I was sent out with an infantry platoon for a few weeks.

As soon as I got back to the base, I knew I wanted to extend my embed for several more months, so a few weeks later, I asked to spend a full deployment with these guys—the full fifteen months. They looked at me as though I were from another planet. "You want to spend fifteen months here? You know what that means, right? That's a long time, and it's even longer here." I told them I understood, and finally, after mountains of paper-work, I was approved. A few months later, the deployment was cut to twelve months. In a way, I was relieved. Covering a war drains you.

Even after being embedded for a year, I couldn't help but feel that I

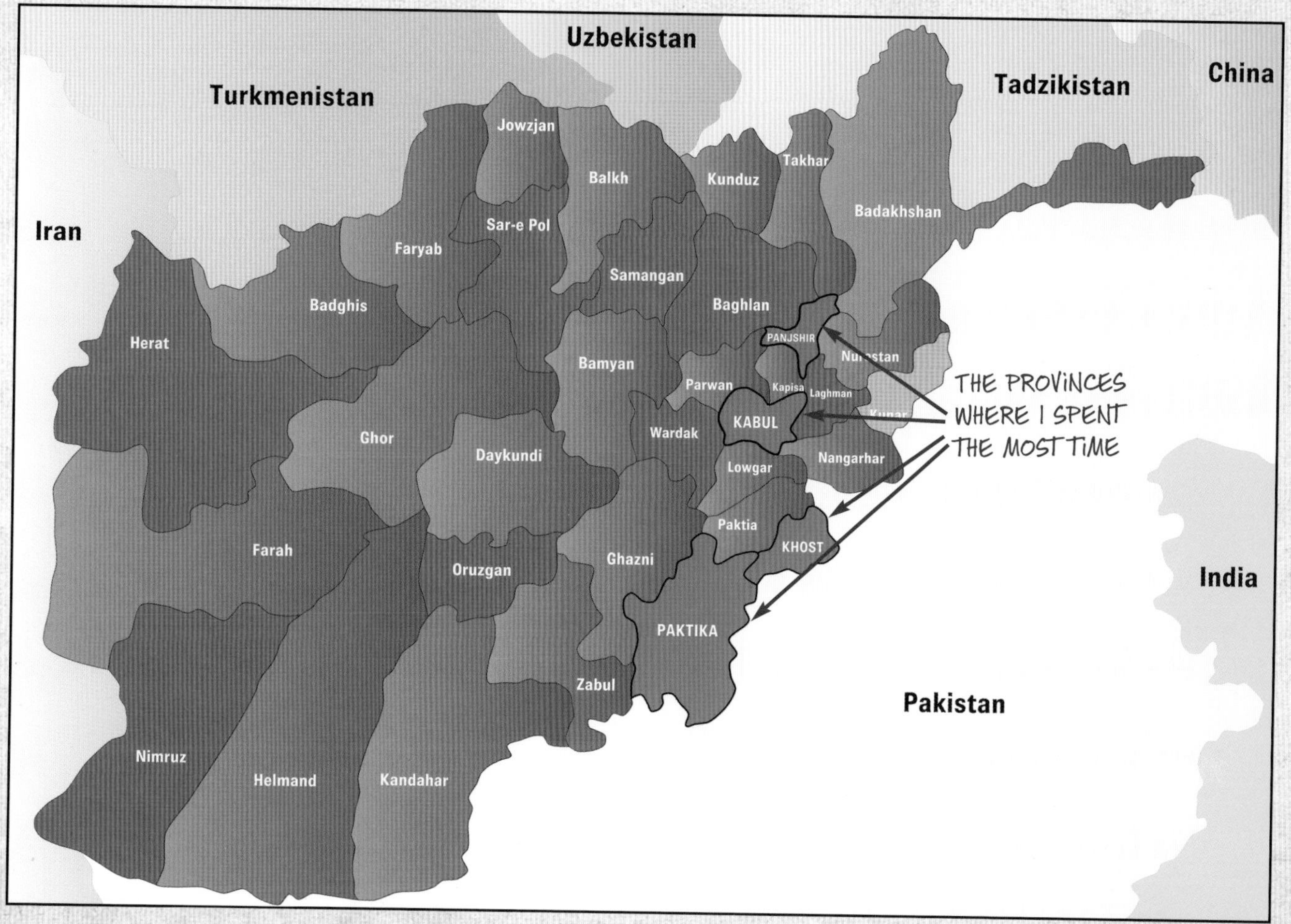
Uzbekistan
Turkmenistan
Tadzikistan
China
Iran
Jowzjan
Balkh
Kunduz
Takhar
Badakhshan
Sar-e Pol
Faryab
Samangan
Badghis
Baghlan
Herat
PANJSHIR
Bamyan
Parwan
Kapisa
Laghman
KABUL
Wardak
Ghor
Daykundi
Lowgar
Nangarhar
Paktia
KHOST
Farah
Oruzgan
Ghazni
PAKTIKA
Zabul
Nimruz
Helmand
Kandahar
India
Pakistan
THE PROVINCES WHERE I SPENT THE MOST TIME

had still seen only one side of Afghanistan's story. Almost as soon as I got home, I decided to go back to cover the other side: civilian life.

And I keep going back. Afghanistan is a part of me now. I'll always find a way to return.

Whenever people learn that I am a photojournalist who spends most of his time in Afghanistan, they ask the same questions: Why do you keep going back? What are you trying to do there? Aren't you scared? How do you do it? Is it worth it? Most of the answers aren't straightforward, even to me.

I have different reasons each time I go back, but my friends there are a big part of why. Not just my friends, actually; it's everyone there. At the same time, I feel lucky to be able to come home to the safety of a place like Canada. The people of Afghanistan don't have that option; they can't just leave. I guess I keep going back because they need a voice. There are so many stories to be told.

I'm not in Afghanistan for political reasons. I'm not trying to find out why the coalition is there; that's an impossible question to get answered. I'm there because I want people to see and feel what it's like to live every day with the war on your doorstep.

Sure, sometimes it's dangerous, and yes, absolutely, I get scared. But when the camera is in front of me, it's like looking through a window. As much as I'm in the situation, I'm somewhat separated from it, and from the fear. I've developed a sense of security by looking at things—no matter what things—from a distance. I know that what I'm seeing is real, but I'm not close enough to actually feel it. I can be hanging out of a helicopter and have no fear at all because, at that moment, I'm thinking like a photographer; I'm considering the composition of the shot, the way the light's falling, the angles in my frame. Take that camera away, though, and fear comes flooding in.

PART 1: EMBEDDED

SPERA DISTRICT, KHOST PROVINCE

I had a close call today. After nearly four months here—embedded with the 101st Airborne Division, 506th Infantry Regiment, 2nd Battalion, Delta Company, 4th Platoon—it could have been my last day in Afghanistan.

We were heading back from a mission to the Pakistan border, five men crowded into each Humvee—an armored truck with a gun turret and bulletproof windows. The trucks look big, but we're crowded in there like sardines. Out on the open road, when the sun beats down on our metal box, it's like wearing full hockey gear and sitting in a sauna—times ten. The armor we wear doesn't breathe at all, plus we wear helmets and gloves (which are fire retardant so that, in case of an explosion, we don't burn our hands; plastic gloves would melt to our skin).

It was a treacherous drive through rough, barren terrain, and the convoy had to move slowly, which made us very easy targets for the Taliban. It's pretty common to get a flat tire, but having to leave the truck to change one makes you vulnerable, so we're careful. If a Humvee breaks down it has to be towed back, and no one wants that.

There are no paved roads, so on the way out we had driven through a wadi—a riverbed that runs through a canyon. Going through a wadi is like whitewater rafting in an armored vehicle. At best we were driving over huge rocks, and at worst we were driving through water high enough to leak into the trucks.

THE TALIBAN—After the collapse of the Communist regime in Afghanistan in 1992, the resulting chaos and bloodshed led to public demands for law and order. In response, a little-known former resistance fighter and religious teacher, Mullah Mohammad Omar, and his taliban (religious students) led a brief but popular campaign to rid southern Afghanistan's Kandahar region of its warlords and bandits. The puritanical Islamist Taliban movement emerged in 1994 and, after a ruthless and effective military campaign, dominated the country from 1996 to 2001. Their victory led to the implementation of shari'a (Islamic law) and transformation of Afghanistan into a safe haven for international terrorist organizations such as al-Qaeda.

On the way back, the lieutenant decided to take the mountain pass instead. It was a very narrow road, dug out of the side of the mountain for one-way traffic. There was no way to make a U-turn. One wrong swerve and you could drop 75 meters (250 feet) straight down.

I was in the lead truck, sitting in the back. It felt like a sandbox in there: every time we went over a bump, dust flew everywhere. It hung thick in the air, catching beams of sunlight.

We'd been out for the whole day, and I had fallen asleep. We were maybe an hour and a half away from the base when I woke up. It felt as if someone had tapped me on the shoulder. I opened my eyes and looked around. My gut was telling me something was wrong. Something bad was about to happen.

The interpreter, a civilian national hired to help the soldiers communicate with the locals, was sitting beside me, still asleep. The three American soldiers up front were quiet but wide awake. I squinted out through the front window, and ahead of us I saw a yellow bag— the kind Afghans use for carrying rice or beans or wheat. It was just plunked there, in the middle of the road, with no one near it.

My heart started beating a little faster as I thought, This isn't right. What's next? I tried to stay calm and focus on what was in front of us, looking around for any threats. Through the window I saw an elderly man standing a bit back from the bag. He looked right at us, then up at the mountain, then back at us.

That's when the gunfire started.

Insurgents were firing at us non-stop from the ridgelines on either side: heavy weapons, rocket-propelled grenades (RPGs), everything. An RPG passed just inches above our truck. We kept going. Up front, Gunner Sergeant Chris Nelson started firing back on both sides, swinging his turret from left to right. I looked to see where he was shooting. On the side of the mountain, I saw puffs of smoke, little clouds of dust—puff, puff, puff—everywhere. I could see where the bullets were hitting but I couldn't see who.

ME WITH AMERICAN SOLDIERS WHO WERE PART OF THE EMBEDDED TRAINING TEAM THAT MENTORS THE AFGHAN NATIONAL ARMY

On this tiny little mountain pass, being attacked from both sides, it was like sitting in a tin can with someone throwing rocks at us. All I could hear was a rapid ding! ding! ding! ding! No one knew where the bullets were going to hit or what

was going to happen next—at least, I didn't. I wasn't trained for this.

The driver stepped on it, trying to get us out of there alive. As I was trying to see out through the haze of dust and smoke, a bullet hit the Humvee's window, inches from my face. I froze—that bulletproof window had just saved my life. But I had to push the thought aside and concentrate on what I was doing; I didn't have time for shock. I knew I wasn't injured, so I just kept photographing and recording audio.

Though it felt like hours, the ambush lasted for only about five minutes. We had no choice but to drive hard and keep moving through it. It took us close to two hours to get back to the compound. That was the longest two hours of my life—we had no way of knowing if there would be more insurgents, or more bombs, waiting on the road ahead.

We all got out okay—no casualties or injuries—but our vehicles were riddled with bullets. Back at the base, most of the soldiers tried to brush off the incident. We stood around joking, talking, and I kept taking photographs.

I noticed a soldier sitting at the Humvee alone. I think he was stunned: maybe he had suddenly realized what had just happened to him, to us, and how lucky we were. I took his photograph through the bullet-riddled glass.

On days like this, I try not to let my thoughts overwhelm me. If I did, I'd be too scared to do my job.

Postscript: Much later, I learned that this soldier, while he was home on leave, committed suicide.

16

SHAMAL DISTRICT, KHOST PROVINCE

In Shamal, searches of Afghan homes are conducted regularly in hopes of finding weapons, explosives, drugs, or money being smuggled by civilians or insurgents. Today I photographed these three obviously scared young boys as they watched a police officer search their home. I can't imagine how it would feel to have armed strangers—foreigners—walk into my home and search it while my father was kept outside, being questioned by police officers.

Sometimes American soldiers are forbidden to go inside on their own to conduct a search; they have to be accompanied by an Afghan police officer. And never are men—foreigners or unrelated Afghan males—allowed to see the women inside. So, during the searches the women are escorted by their husbands from room to room, and everybody is

Different Islamic interpretations of men's and women's roles account for some of the variation in the treatment of women across Muslim countries. Under the Taliban's interpretation, women were stripped of their rights, but in many other Muslim countries, women can have a great deal of power. The Quran says that men and women are equal before God and in their religious duties and that neither sex is superior, but it also makes men financially responsible for their wives.

The Quran instructs both male and female Muslims to dress modestly. The wearing of veils, known as hijab, or a conservative robe that covers the entire head but not the face, known as a chador, has been imposed on female Muslims in many countries. How much of themselves women should cover is open to interpretation, and the Afghan Taliban enforce the strictest interpretation possible. In private, in the company of their husbands and close family members, women can remove their headscarves.

supposed to turn their backs as they pass. It's astonishing to me. How do they know the women aren't smuggling things from place to place? Or that these aren't men disguised as women? After all, they're completely covered up.

Where the searches are conducted depends on the area, the village, and the information the NATO forces get. Sometimes it's a whole area, a large section marked off on a map, in which every house is gone through. Today it had been reported that insurgents were moving through this particular area, which is known to be pro-Taliban and is near the site of a suicide bombing that killed a lot of people a few months earlier. The soldiers had heard that the Taliban were using the houses as safe places to stash weapons, explosives, narcotics, money—anything they could smuggle across the border to keep them going.

The insurgents often booby-trap the houses or the caches. The houses are usually pretty dark—few homes outside the cities have electricity—so the authorities approach everything with caution. Sometimes, as soon as they touch something or move it, it will explode.

Today was a good day—no booby traps, or anything else, were found in these houses.

NATO FORCES—Since al-Qaeda was using Afghanistan as a safe haven from which to launch terrorist attacks against the West, an international coalition led by the United States invaded the country on October 7, 2001. That same year, under a United Nations Security Council mandate known as Resolution 1386, the North Atlantic Treaty Organization (NATO) became involved, establishing the International Security Assistance Force (ISAF), a multi-nation military force whose task was to stabilize Afghanistan. In 2010 the ISAF consisted of 48 nations contributing a total of 131,730 personnel. These forces maintain 27 provincial reconstruction teams that help to provide security and support the development and sustainability of the Afghan government.

SPERA DISTRICT, KHOST PROVINCE

A man cradling his dying daughter came into the base today. A young American medic who had been trying to save the girl's life followed behind them. They had been driving for hours, searching for help. The man was okay with my taking his picture, so, although it was a very difficult moment to photograph, I ultimately decided I should capture it. Maybe it gave him some hope, too, knowing that people might see the photo and that it might help prevent someone else's child from suffering.

The girl had breathing problems and the Afghan soldiers didn't have the proper tools to open the oxygen tanks that could save her. The American lieutenant tried to call for a medevac (medical evacuation) helicopter to take her to a hospital, but they wouldn't send one out just for one dying young girl.

The lieutenant went with his only other option. He would take the girl and her father to the nearest medical facility in an armored vehicle; all traffic stops for armored vehicles, which would save them valuable time. Even so, they had a two-hour drive ahead.

As soon as they got into the truck, the girl stopped breathing. The young medic started CPR (cardiopulmonary resuscitation) and continued for a long time. She was already gone, but the medic didn't stop trying to save her. He didn't want to let her go. He talked about it afterward, obviously shaken; it must have been one of the harder moments of his deployment.

It was heartbreaking for everybody. A young child had died in front of us, and there was nothing we could do. To see a girl's life vanish before your eyes when you know she could have survived in other circumstances just overwhelms you with grief. Today it didn't matter what uniform anyone was wearing or what god we prayed to. Sorrow connected us all and stripped everything else away.

This young girl had nothing to do with the conflict, but everything to do with what's wrong in Afghanistan.

AFGHAN SOLDIERS—In May 2002, international efforts to create an Afghan National Army (ANA) from scratch began in earnest. To reduce Afghans' concerns about the army's ethnic makeup, the goal was to build an army that was 42 percent Pashtun, 27 percent Tajik, 9 percent Uzbek, 9 percent Hazara, and 13 percent other cultural groups. Maintaining this balance remains a challenge. The number of ANA troops is currently around 112,000, and the goal is to raise that number to 240,000 by 2014.

A young Afghan soldier was brought into the combat support hospital today in Camp Salerno, near the Pakistan border. His vehicle had struck a roadside bomb. Most patients being brought in are Afghans—civilians, soldiers, police officers. Coalition forces use the hospital, too, but you see many more Afghans coming in because they don't have the proper equipment to protect them.

Striking a bomb in a regular pickup truck is devastating.

Coalition forces all have well-equipped armored vehicles, but roadside bombs, or IEDs (improvised explosive devices), still damage them and kill people. Some of these bombs are designed to blow up tanks. Imagine what one of them would do to a regular pickup truck, which is all that most of the Afghan forces have. No wonder so many more Afghans are injured or killed.

In ten months, the hospital's fifty-person staff, made up of members of the American military, treated more than 485 patients from the five surrounding provinces. Trying to save these patients is traumatic for the air force nurses, soldiers and officers, and doctors, who are often young. Air force deployments are six months long; I've spent only a month at this hospital and have witnessed some of the most horrific things I've ever seen.

The corridors are filled with screaming adults and young children, injured by bombs that were dropped in the wrong place or that malfunctioned. They are forever scarred, physically and emotionally, because of something completely beyond their control. No photograph or even video can do justice to the horrors and tragedies of these emergency rooms. The smells, the sounds, the chaos—it's impossible to describe. It's like being in hell.

Amid all of this, men and women do amazing work saving lives, saving limbs, and giving people hope. When the injured come through that hospital door, whether friend or foe, they are all treated the same. Inside these walls, your uniform, the color of your skin, your religion—none of that matters. That's rare in this war.

A VIEW OUT THE BACK OF AN AMERICAN MILITARY CHINOOK HELICOPTER FLYING OVER KHOST PROVINCE

BERMEL DISTRICT, PAKTIKA PROVINCE

Today I spent the day in an Afghan bazaar, a market, along the Pakistani border. American soldiers patrol the streets there, watching the Kuchis. Kuchis are nomadic families who usually keep livestock and travel with it throughout Afghanistan and Pakistan. The soldiers keep a close eye on them in this area, since some are known to be Taliban-friendly, and the Kuchis' lifestyle makes it easy for them to smuggle weapons, equipment, and drugs.

The bazaar is more than just a market, really; it's a gathering place. Recently a Taliban fighter was killed in a firefight—a shootout with American soldiers.

American military intelligence and Afghan police officers took his body to a district center, where officials searched his clothing. They looked for identification, cellphones, notes, or phone numbers, anything that could lead to more information about weapons caches or insurgents' plans. They found a government voter-registration card on this man, and a cellphone. This guy was a Taliban fighter and he had a government voter-registration card, which means he could have walked into any polling station. He had the means to attack from the inside.

Once the examination was finished, the Afghan police brought the fighter's body to this market. They placed it on a military stretcher with a white cloth over it, and then a foil warming blanket, the kind you see at car accidents, on top of that. The officials knew, this being an insurgent-friendly place, that the villagers would get word to the Taliban to come and take care of their own and give the man a proper burial.

Later the police officers told us that people had approached and thrown money at the body (it would be collected and given to the family of the deceased). Then they carried the corpse through the market, believing that the dead man was a martyr who had died for a just cause. The soldiers patrolling the area could only watch in frustration. There was clear support for the insurgency here.

Today I was with a group of American-embedded training-team soldiers close to Bermel. The Americans are here to mentor and train the Afghan army.

We went out to a village on a humanitarian aid drop. The Afghan and American soldiers handed out blankets, food, books, pens, and any type of medical supplies that people needed. These sorts of missions are pretty frequent—maybe once every one to three weeks, depending on the area and the unit.

A group of young kids gathered instantly. The elders, who take all the donations and distribute them evenly among village members, told them to stay back, so the kids just lined up along the rocks. They watched quietly as the soldiers handed out the supplies.

This started out as one of my happier days in Afghanistan. There was a different vibe in the air;

we actually saw smiles from some of the children and elders. The barriers, for once, were down. It was a really nice feeling.

It didn't last long. As soon as we left, a group of insurgents was spotted on the mountain ridgeline near the area, and within fifteen minutes artillery strikes had started coming in. On the way back to the base, all I heard were explosions, and I could see smoke rising from the mountaintop.

Another day in Afghanistan.

AN AFGHAN CHILD WAVES TO AN AMERICAN CONVOY

31

32

SHAMAL DISTRICT, KHOST PROVINCE

The vast majority of Afghans are Muslims, and devout Muslims pray five times a day. The evening prayer, or Salatu-l-'Isha, is the last prayer of the day, and it takes place when the sun is going down. I was in the police headquarters today as Afghan officers in the Shamal district put aside their assault rifles, their AK-47s, to pray.

Everywhere across the country, Afghans— soldiers, civilians, Taliban—were doing the same thing, united in prayer but divided by what it means. The foreign soldiers try to be respectful of these rituals.

Afghan police officers who stay on the army base use one of the rooms where they live and sleep as a prayer room. A mosque is still being built. It was almost completed once before, but it was destroyed by a suicide bomber. The mosque was collateral damage— it wasn't targeted; it just happened to be on the base that was.

The followers of Islam, who are called Muslims, believe in one God, Allah, and they believe that the Islamic prophet Muhammad was God's last prophet. The first guide to a Muslim's life is the holy Quran, the book the Prophet Muhammad presented to the world.

Islam is based on five principles, known as the five pillars of Islam, that shape the lives of Muslims: (1) *shahada*, the testimony of faith; (2) *salah*, the daily ritual of prayer; (3) *zakat*, payment of the alms tax, which is charity for the poor and less fortunate; (4) *sawm*, the practice of fasting to move closer to God; and (5) the *hajj*, a pilgrimage to Mecca (in Saudi Arabia) that all Muslims who are able to must make at least once. Almost all Muslims belong to one of the two major denominations, the Sunni or the Shi'a. In contemporary Afghanistan, approximately 80 percent of the population is Sunni and 19 percent is Shi'a.

KHOST-GARDEZ PASS

I joined some members of the Afghan National Police on patrol today in an area not far from Shamal where chromite is mined. Chromite is a valuable mineral used for making stainless steel. Some villagers believe that these mines belong to them and not the government. They can make a lot of money mining the chromite for themselves and smuggling it into Pakistan to sell.

To stop the smuggling, checkpoints are staffed by private security forces hired by the government, but it's hard to monitor. There are checkpoints along the Khost-Gardez Pass—the most vital route between Khost and Kabul.

I took this picture just as arguing broke out between some of the village elders and the government-hired security staff, who were preventing the chromite from being taken out. We showed up as the village elder was saying, "I have three hundred guys ready to fight and kill for this chromite. It's ours."

The lieutenant of the platoon I was with was skeptical. He tried to explain diplomatically to the elder that the security men were part of the government and that the chromite wasn't going anywhere.

The elder got angry and repeated what he'd already said: "Listen. If

A TALIBAN AMMUNITION POUCH CAPTURED BY AMERICAN SOLDIERS AND GIVEN TO ME AS A GIFT

these chromite guys don't leave, you are going to be attacked."

The lieutenant stood his ground and replied, "Well, they aren't leaving, so you do what you've got to do."

The next thing I knew, gunfire was exploding from over the ridgeline. We were surrounded. Everybody scrambled to jump into the trucks and get out of there. The chromite security guys got into position to start fighting, just as gunfire erupted from another part of the hill—non-stop gunfire.

PRIVATE SECURITY CONTRACTORS—
The presence of private security contractors (PSCs) in Afghanistan came out of the need to protect the highways and the commercial trucking firms that carry goods along Afghanistan's main routes. In 2010, the Afghan Ministry of the Interior reported that 52 licensed private security companies were operating in Afghanistan, collectively employing 25,000 armed guards as escorts for the tons of cargo required by NATO and U.S. forces. In addition there are hundreds of unregistered private security providers, most of which are Afghan-owned and -operated.

It was clearly an ambush: on every peak, on every ridgeline of the mountains around us, men armed with AK-47s were shooting at us.

We got back to the army compound safely, with the security guys. The lieutenant called his superiors to report what had happened. He then tried to send out the Afghan police, but they wouldn't go. They said it was none of their business, not their problem: "You Americans are involved. You go take care of it." The lieutenant called his superiors again, but they said there was nothing they could do. American forces were not supposed to get involved in local matters, and this conflict was a green-on-green issue, which means Afghan-on-Afghan. Everyone seemed to think someone else should be dealing with it.

But how is the government supposed to deal with it when the security they hire gets chased out? Soon that checkpoint won't even exist, and smuggling and who knows what else—transporting weapons or drugs, Taliban fighters making their way across the border—will go on unchecked.

So what's next? Are they going to keep fighting? Who has the right to control the area? It's a muddled, never-ending cycle. All these impossible-to-enforce rules, all this troubled warfare, and so much money involved. It's a mess.

SHAMAL DISTRICT, KHOST PROVINCE

A few days ago, the platoon I was with was called out as a Quick Response Force for another platoon that was being ambushed by a very large band of Taliban fighters. These situations are always tense, and I have to cut any feelings I have about them entirely out of the equation. I have to focus on where I should be and what's going on around me. Some days it's harder to do that than others.

The ambush was up in the mountains, near the forests. We got up there shortly after it ended, and it was an awful scene. A number of Afghan police officers and one American lieutenant had been killed. Several other officers and soldiers lay bloodied and hurt. Disabled trucks were smoking and riddled with bullet holes. The Taliban did a lot of damage that day.

These young Afghan police officers, some injured by shrapnel, were waiting to be airlifted

out. That would be no small feat—we ended up stuck in the area for three days, surrounded by insurgents.

At night, coalition artillery and bombs were dropping constantly. I heard that a lot of insurgents were killed. It was scary; out in the mountains it was pitch dark all around, and I kept hearing over my headphones that we were completely surrounded. We barely slept, just dozing off when we could in the back of a Humvee. When I had to step outside the vehicle to pee, I couldn't see a thing. I didn't know if someone was suddenly going to come around a corner or from behind a bush and shoot me or stab me. I just didn't know.

Finally the trucks and equipment were taken apart and lifted out by helicopter. During the days, the platoon concentrated on getting the men and all the gear out of there, keeping things secure, making sure everyone in the area was safe. Helicopters came and went and other platoons rolled in. The Afghan police officers were airlifted out, and minutes later we left, too. I drove out with a number of American soldiers and Afghan police officers, and it took several hours. Even though it was daylight and we could see, it was still an incredibly nerve-wracking trip.

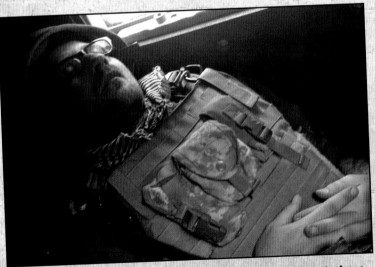

ME PASSED OUT IN THE BACK OF A HUMVEE

HOUSING UNIT AT AMERICAN FORWARD OPERATING BASE CLARK KHOST PROVINCE

BALLISTIC COMBAT GLASSES TO PROTECT YOUR EYES IN CASE OF AN EXPLOSION

Last night I was in my hut with five or six other soldiers, in a housing unit at American Forward Operating Base Clark. It was about nine o'clock. I was wrapping things up, thinking about getting ready for bed. I was sitting in my bunk, a computer on my lap, looking over the day's work. Suddenly I heard this deafening sound overhead, as if a jet were landing right on the roof. A split second later, I heard the explosion. Another split second later, I felt it.

Everything happened in a blur. The backpack holding my cameras, hard drives, and passport—everything I need to make it out of the country with my work—always stays by the door, right next to my body armor and helmet. In a blink I

was dressed, armor somewhat on, back-pack over my shoulder, running toward a bunker. Because so many rocket attacks, suicide bombings, and smaller-arms attacks occur on bases, we always have to be ready to flee.

It was pitch black outside. The base is kept dark at night because lights give the Taliban something to aim at. I could hear panic in the air, people running around, yelling, making sure everybody was accounted for.

I booked it toward that bunker, following voices and footsteps but without a clear idea of the direction I was supposed to be going. A rocket could have hit right beside me, or maybe even under me. I just kept running blindly into the dark, hoping that the bunker was near.

The rocket had landed about 50 meters (150 feet) from where I was staying, hitting an empty building that was under construction. We sat in the bunker for a few hours while the army secured the area. They ordered mountain patrols around the base to make sure the area was all clear.

Huddled around one dim red light in the bunker, some people told jokes, others played cards, some slept or listened to their iPods. It was kind of like when a machine breaks down at a factory—a small break for the workers for a couple of hours. It's surreal, but this becomes a part of daily life. Despite the panic, shock, and fear, you have to laugh at it to get by. We sit in the bunker for a few hours, we go back, we fall asleep. We just keep going.

OPERATION PIRATES COVE, SHAMAL DISTRICT, KHOST PROVINCE

My last mission with the American soldiers has ended. It was their last mission, too. I feel great, extremely relieved that I am going home soon, that all of us are going home. We'll get to see our families; our lives will go back to normal. I am happy to be alive, to have all my limbs, and to have survived the year.

This final mission took three days. In a convoy with Afghan National Army soldiers, we headed to an area where an insurgent with a vehicle full of explosives had recently driven into a military compound, killing himself and many others. The Taliban use suicide bombers in much the same way that coalition forces drop bombs—they're just another weapon. That bombing killed sixteen people and injured even more. It forced the platoon I was with to abandon its area of operations and retreat to a larger base.

The Central Intelligence Agency and Special Forces found out where the bomb had been built and who was involved. During this last combat operation with 4th Platoon, we headed to that area with Special Forces to collect evidence and destroy any remaining buildings used by the Taliban.

I accompanied the soldiers as they spent the first day of the mission searching villages and looking for explosives, weapons, any sign of insurgents or their paraphernalia. That night I slept in the back of one of the trucks because there was snow everywhere.

AMERICAN SPECIAL FORCES WAIT FOR THE DUST AND SMOKE TO CLEAR DURING THE OPERATION

In the morning, I started taking photographs, but it was weird because people were smiling; they were relieved, I guess, that the mission was nearly done. Some Afghan soldiers blasted music out of a truck. They laid their weapons on the ground and danced in circles for almost an hour, non-stop. Afterward, everybody sat around drinking chai. I had no interpreter, but someone spoke a bit of English and I had picked up a few

words in Dari, one of Afghanistan's official languages, so I got by. We found a way to understand each other.

On the last morning, the platoon got its orders to destroy any remaining buildings. Leveling these places is the only way to make sure insurgents don't use them later. So the soldiers and the Special Forces troops threw grenades and opened fire with their heavy weapons. The buildings, made out of wood and mud, went down like a stack of cards in a breeze. Over the explosions, I could hear the soldiers cheering and celebrating. By the end of the day, there was nothing left but a big cloud of dust hanging over us.

This mission was more laid-back than most of the others I've been on. We had non-stop air surveillance overhead, so everybody knew no insurgents were nearby. On the last night, we sat by campfires and just hung out, enjoying one another's company, as if we were on a glorified camping trip! We felt we could finally stop and take a breath, knowing that, for the moment, every-body was safe.

On the way out I boarded a Chinook helicopter along with the Afghan and American soldiers. Riding in a helicopter can be pretty intense. It swoops up and dives down without warning, jolting you every which way, and tilts at crazy angles, maneuvering whichever way it has to to avoid being fired on. Often a couple of gunners are on board—one in the front, one in the rear. These guys fly with the windows and hatch open most of the time. In winter it gets crazy cold in these helicopters. I layer myself with gloves, toques, and double or triple pants sometimes.

Tonight, back at the base, everyone has started packing up for home. The atmosphere is almost giddy, we're all so happy to be leaving, so relieved to have survived.

Home. I can't wait to get there. Just to wear my normal clothes again, to go out for a drive in my car. It's been a year since I've driven, and I miss the freedom of it. I miss a lot of the freedoms I have at home; this past year has made me realize how grateful I am to have them.

CULTURE SHOCK

Coming home after being embedded with the American forces for a year was hard. The culture shock happened in reverse—it hit me when I got back.

Driving on a familiar stretch of highway near my house, I'd look up at ridgelines, thinking of ambushes. Ambushes aren't my reality back home, of course, but that fear had become so set in my mind after living with it for twelve months that it was hard to stop bracing for one after I left.

Even after being back for months, whenever a door slammed or I heard a loud noise, my heart started pounding. I'm really jumpy still. Being over there for so long has changed me. I try to deal with it as best I can, but I'm not sure if I really know yet how I've been affected. It's tough to talk about. I never tell strangers where I've been—I don't want to be questioned.

Part of me felt guilty coming back, knowing what was happening in Afghanistan every day. Here I was, enjoying my simple freedoms, while my friends suffered. That didn't feel right.

One day near the end of my twelve months, I was sitting with an Afghan friend, talking. He was an interpreter for the American army. He asked me if I was happy to be going home. I said I was, extremely happy. I said that I missed my family, my friends. I told him I missed the little, everyday things like driving to the corner store or going to get groceries without carrying identification or worrying about a suicide bomber or an ambush. "I won't have to wake up to explosions anymore," I told him. "I won't have to wear my armor anymore! I won't have to live in fear."

He nodded. "Yeah. That will be nice."

It hit me hard. Here I was going on about leaving when my friend couldn't. He didn't have the option of picking up and going home; he was home.

I knew then that I would go back. I'd seen the military side; now I wanted to see the civilian side, the human side. This time I would go on my own.

A CAMERA THAT DIED ON ME IN AFGHANISTAN AFTER SIX MONTHS OF USE

Part 2:
Another Day in Afghanistan

KABUL

About two and a half months after the embed, I was at home, looking at my work, dissatisfied: something was missing. I still didn't have a good understanding of how Afghan civilians felt about the war or how it affected their daily lives. I felt a pull to go back that I couldn't ignore; there was still so much going on that needed to be documented.

There was no military to help me arrange things this time, so I talked to friends and acquaintances who might know of a place I could stay. I ended up settling at the Mustafa Hotel in Kabul. It's not a UN-approved hotel; after security in the capital deteriorated, a lot

THE CITY OF KABUL

Nurestan

Kunar

Laghman

Kabul

Nangarhar

Lowgar

Paktia

Khost

Pakistan

Paktika

of people stopped staying here. But even with the occasional lack of heat and hot water, and a ceiling peppered with bullet holes from wild parties, I feel comfortable here. After a few weeks I got to know the staff. Coming back to my room at the end of the day is like coming back to good friends; I trust them, and they look out for me and my stuff. I've also met lots of other guests—backpackers, civilians, other photojournalists, military contractors—who use the Mustafa as their home base, too.

Today's Friday—the Muslim day of rest—and I got back to the hotel late after spending the day at Qargha Lake. It was packed, as it is most Fridays. People flock there on their days off, taking their families out in colored paddle boats or going horseback riding.

There's even a golf course nearby. It's nice to see people really let go.

It's funny that with so much war and so much history of war in this country, people still pay money to shoot pellet guns as they try to hit balloons, playing the same game we play at fairs in North America. It strikes me how similar we are, even though people back home think Afghanistan is so far away and that the Afghan people are so different.

Qargha Lake is spectacular. The air is fresh and you're surrounded by mountains. Open-sided fabric tents are set up on raised wooden platforms with colorful carpets strewn about. People are everywhere, picnicking, swimming, just enjoying life—and maybe, for the moment, forgetting about everything else that's going on.

The craziest thing is the swing ride—just like the ones at fairs in North America. Well, sort of. My buddies, Afghan guys from Kabul who interpret for the American military, dragged me onto it. I was nervous—the thing runs on a lawnmower motor! There are no safety regulations like the ones we have back home.

So I was sitting on this thing as it started swinging higher and higher, holding tight to the railing in front of me because there were no safety belts or bars. It was worse than I'd imagined—I was positive I was going to fall out. The pole at the top was totally rusted out and the ride squeaked with every sway. The operator kept pulling the pole, spinning the motor faster. I thought it would never stop.

When I did finally get on firm ground again, my friends couldn't stop laughing at me.

It was a good day, filled with a sense of normalcy and hope that's hard to find in Afghanistan. When I walked around with my camera, nobody questioned it. People were just going on with their lives. I could almost have convinced myself there was no conflict going on, if the reminders hadn't been so close by. We drove out amid discarded tanks and through a refugee camp.

And even on Fridays, insurgents still set off bombs and suicide bombers still attack. Driving home, it wouldn't have been unusual to hear an explosion—background noise to the end of a beautiful day.

KABUL

You can always find something going on in Afghanistan on a Friday. My friend and I were out for a walk today when we came upon a swimming pool. He asked me if I wanted to go check it out. Summers aren't awfully humid in Afghanistan but they are very hot. Only a few buildings are air-conditioned, so a swim seemed like a good idea.

No women or girls were allowed at the pool—just men. My friend, who is an Afghan interpreter, asked if I would be allowed to photograph and was told it was no problem. As usual, when I first brought my camera out, a small crowd gathered. I told them what I was doing and why I was there—that I wanted to show daily life during this time in Kabul's history. Everyone was very welcoming.

We stayed the afternoon, drinking chai with the owners and some Afghan police officers who had come in to swim, to cool off a little bit. Police officers and soldiers are still on duty on Fridays, of course. War doesn't just stop on the day of rest.

We sat around, chatting about Afghanistan and how things were going, about some of their problems and how they saw their future. The officers talked about their frustration with checkpoints. At these checkpoints they are supposed to be in charge of directing civilians. Foreign army convoys often patrol the areas, too, and the police officers complained that the soldiers in the convoys just do whatever they like. A soldier might start yelling at an officer guarding the checkpoint, disregarding that officer's authority. Being belittled like that makes the police officer look like a fool in front of his own people, and they lose respect for him. The officer, in turn, resents the foreign soldiers.

A lot of men feel they are unable to fight their own fight. In their own country, they don't have the authority they need to get things done.

DINNER WITH FARHAD

KABUL

In North America, guys might get together to play golf or watch a fight in their spare time. In Kabul it's much the same, except the golf course is all sand and the fight is between dogs.

Before the invasion by the coalition forces, the Kabul Golf Course had been closed and used as a Taliban outpost—a small base they could operate out of, sleep and eat in, and use as a staging area for planning missions. In 2003 it reopened to the public. It's used mostly by foreigners now, but some locals do go there to play.

The green is not green, it's brown and dusty. I noticed old Russian tanks all over the place. Everywhere the Afghans look, they are reminded not just of the current conflict but also of previous ones.

Even a favorite sport—dog fighting—is about conflict. Every Friday there are at least a couple of dogfights around Kabul. Hundreds of people go. Dogfights were banned when the Taliban ruled, but they are making a comeback now.

Under Islam, dogs are considered unclean animals, and Muslims are not allowed to keep one inside the house. The presence of a dog inside a house would make prayers said there of no value and render the room impure for ritual purposes. Afghans traditionally use dogs to help with farm work, hunting, or guarding livestock, crops, and property, but these dogs are kept outside the home at all times. An exception is made for Muslims who need a guide dog, which can be kept inside but should sleep separately from the people in the home. Neither dog fighting nor gambling are permitted under Islamic law; however, dog-fighting matches, and variations that pit other animals against one another, have been documented throughout Afghanistan's history.

These fights are entertainment, a distraction, and the atmosphere is frenetic and exciting. Vendors sell snacks; dice games are played for cash. An announcer gets the crowd going, and once the owners have decided which dogs will fight, they just let them go at each other.

The dogs never fight to the death. The handlers always pull them apart once the referee sees that one animal is dominating the other. Trainers and owners are always present at these fights, pulling the dogs apart, pouring water on them. A winning dog is worth a lot of money.

As brutal as the sport looks, it's not much different from boxing. Huge amounts of money are bet on the fighters. At one match, someone lost a US$20,000 SUV. At another match I went to, $10,000 was wagered. That's serious money when you consider that the average wage in Afghanistan is $100 a month.

Dogfights attract people from all walks of life—regular citizens, politicians, even warlords.

WARLORDS—Warlords is a term used to describe unofficial power brokers who dominate territory by maintaining large private armies and controlling political offices. The evolution of warlord groups in Afghanistan reflects the militarization of Afghan society and the resources available to the resistance. Warlord organizations usually focus on illegal activities such as narcotics production, trafficking in weapons and drugs, and "taxing" the residents in their territory or those who use the roadways under their control.

warlords are criminals with their own armies, and when they're at a fight, everyone knows it. They are often revered and well respected by regular Afghans, maybe because, despite their illegal activities and affiliations, they do give back to their communities—donating money, dealing with crime, providing health care, and even mediating land disputes. They also build mosques and schools, and in doing so, they generate work for the locals. When warlords come to a fight with their dogs, they generally run the show.

Accidents can happen at these events. Last Friday we drove to a dogfight that a friend of mine (also a reporter) wanted to check out. He went down to the arena to watch the fight up close; I stayed back in the crowd, looking for something different to photograph.

I came across a dog that was chained up and sleeping. There was a pathway behind him, and it looked as though I could walk past him. But as soon as I was behind him, he sprang up and sank his teeth right into my left leg. I leapt back and shook him off. Thankfully, the dog let go.

I stumbled down to the arena, yelling at my friend about what had just happened. My leg started to feel funny. I gingerly lifted my pant leg and saw blood everywhere. I grabbed my friend and said, "Dude, let's go. We have to go to the hospital. I've got to get some rabies shots."

It took three hospitals before we found one with rabies vaccine. Finally a doctor saw me, looked over the bite, disinfected it, and patched me up. It cost about US$150 for the vaccine. The first round was given to me at the hospital, and for the four rounds after that I went to a pharmacy. I'll have a scar on my leg now—a permanent reminder to be a lot more careful around those dogs.

KABUL ZOO

I took this shot at the zoo—
a popular spot, and famous
for housing the only pig in
Afghanistan. The pig typically
draws large crowds—people are
fascinated by it. Because
Afghanistan is predominently
Muslim, pork is forbidden, so
most people have never seen
a pig in their lives.

Similar to other religions, Islam restricts some foods. Acceptable foods are called *halal*; forbidden ones are called *haram*. The pig is the only animal that is especially forbidden in Islam; pork and all pork products are considered *haram* regardless of how the pigs are killed or prepared. The pig is considered an unclean animal, and the instruction about pork being *haram* is found in the *Quran* in at least four places. Other *haram* foods are blood, carrion, meat from animals that have been improperly slaughtered, and alcohol. Pigs have long disappeared from Afghanistan's landscape; the Kabul Zoo is home to the last live one, a male named *khunzir*, an Arabic term meaning "pig."

KABUL

Today is Eid al-Adha (the Festival of Sacrifice), which signals the end of the **hajj**—the ritual pilgrimage to Mecca—all over the Muslim world. During Eid, families that can afford to do so buy an animal to sacrifice. The animals are shared three ways: within the family, with neighbors, and with the poor. The men distribute the meat to the poor; they hand it out at refugee camps and to homeless people on the street.

Eid is an important celebration. Families dress up, and some boys even wear suits. It's probably the best they look all year. A whole family, including the women, gathers to sacrifice the animal—usually a cow, goat, or sheep. I saw this ritual taking place all over the village. I walked through the streets, which were completely free of traffic, taking in the festivities. For the first time that I can remember, I didn't have a film of dust in my mouth from cars whizzing by.

Today was one of my more amazing days in Afghanistan. I've never seen Kabul so alive with celebration. Kids playing, everybody happy. Afghans deserve to live every day the way they did today.

Once a year, Muslims have an opportunity to participate in the *hajj*, a pilgrimage to Mecca, a holy city located in Saudi Arabia. *Hajj* is the fifth pillar of Islam, and the Quran dictates that every able Muslim man and woman must make a pilgrimage to Mecca at least once. Exceptions are granted to those who are sick or mentally handicapped, and women who have no husbands or male relatives to escort them.

During the *hajj*, about two million Muslims arrive in Mecca and perform rituals together around the Masjid al-Haram (the Holy Mosque), which contains the Ka'ba, a cubical stone structure that Muslims believe was built by Ibrahim and his son Ismail. At the end of the *hajj*, Muslims throughout the world celebrate the holiday of Eid al-Adha, on the tenth day of the twelfth month of the Islamic calendar. The festival honors the Prophet Ibrahim's willingness to sacrifice his own son if asked to by Allah, and Muslims slaughter an animal to remind them of life's sacredness. During the holiday, Muslims attend mosques, visit family and friends, and exchange gifts.

PAGHMAN DISTRICT, KABUL

Driving through Paghman today, right by Qargha Lake, I saw some farmers working in their wheat fields. Agriculture is very important in Afghanistan; that's how most people sustain themselves. They grow all kind of things: grapes, almonds, melons, cotton, corn, rice, potatoes, barley, and lots of wheat. It's all done by hand or with animals. I haven't seen any industrial farm machines.

I asked the driver to stop the car, and he pulled over. This farmer looked up at me and saw my camera. I nodded my head to ask if it was okay. We had no verbal exchange, but I could tell by his body language and gestures that it was fine for me to photograph him. I've been a photographer for a long time, and being able to read people is just something that I've picked up along the way. But you don't have to be a photographer to know when people are comfortable around you and are willing to let you into their lives.

PANJSHIR VALLEY, PANJSHIR PROVINCE

I love spending time in Panjshir province—it's an amazing, peaceful place. The road there is smooth and newly paved. It's such a relief, because most of the time I'm bumping along on unfinished roads, pothole after pothole. They aren't even roads, really, just paths through a desert.

Panjshir is about a three-hour drive north of Kabul, through the Shomali Plains. As we enter the area, we have to register at a checkpoint—another reminder of the war. Because the area is very anti-Taliban, security is a bit more relaxed. The American soldiers go out with just a rifle—no helmet, no body armor.

The river that runs through the area is clean, gentle, and serene, with mountains for a glorious backdrop. It's no more beautiful than scenery I've seen driving through North America, I guess, but all the chaos going on elsewhere in Afghanistan makes Panjshir's loveliness much more striking.

I went with a friend to visit his family. I watched one guy climb a tree and shake its delicious cherries into

a net below. Along the river's edge I photographed men fishing, and I tried it myself. We spent a very relaxing hour listening to the rushing water. For a little while we could forget about the war. Nobody cared that I was a foreigner. Even though I was in Western clothes, nobody looked at me twice.

Panjshir is paradise, except for one thing. As soon as you drive into the area, you see decrepit Russian tanks and old Russian artillery littering the sides of the highways and the farmers' fields. Such images bring back the reality of living in Afghanistan: stark reminders lingering on the shores of the river, beauty bordered by ugliness.

ONE OF MANY OLD RUSSIAN
BOMBS ALONG THE HIGHWAY

THE RUSSIAN OCCUPATION:
DEC 24, 1979 – FEB 15, 1989

The worst blow to the stability and prosperity of Afghanistan was when the Union of Soviet Socialist Republics (USSR) invaded the country in 1979. The Soviet Army was trying to help the ruling Communist government in Kabul suppress a popular uprising against it. The mujahideen resistance groups received anti-Communist support from neighboring Pakistan, and later from the United States, Saudi Arabia, and Egypt, which secretly supplied them with weapons and money. In an effort to crush the growing rebellion, the Soviet military caused widespread destruction of irrigation systems, villages, and livestock. In 1989 the Geneva Accord ended the war and the Soviets withdrew, but by then between one and two million Afghans had been killed, more than five million had fled Afghanistan, and three million had been wounded. Countless landmines remained buried in the countryside, leaving a cruel legacy that lasted long after the war was over.

In 1991, when the Soviet Union collapsed, its financial assistance to Afghanistan also ended. The international support for Afghan resistance groups ended soon after, as did international political interest in the country. Over the next three years, rival groups and warlords fought each other for political dominance, until a small but effective band of religious students, known as the Taliban, rose to power.

KABUL

During my time in Afghanistan, I've been to lots of political campaign rallies. They're huge events in Afghanistan, and often chaotic to photograph. People get very excited; massive crowds follow the campaign vehicles, chasing after them to the main roads. It's more like a party.

Presidential rallies are usually held in stadiums or some other kind of large gathering place. Security is very high. Everybody dances and plays instruments and yells and sings and has an amazing time—except for the women. The women are always pushed to the sides, into their own little sections. They're not allowed to go into the fields or the celebratory areas. Sometimes separate rallies are held specifically for women, who are allowed to vote but are mostly told who to vote for by their husbands.

Afghanistan has had many different systems of government. It has been a monarchy, under kings known as emirs or shahs; a republic; and a theocracy, in which a religious group, the Taliban, held power. In 2003 Afghanistan became a republic once again, with three branches of government: the executive, the legislative, and the judicial. In 2004 the country held its first presidential election, and Hamid Karzai (see opposite page, center figure) was sworn in for a five-year term as president. He appointed several women to his cabinet, and the first female governor in Afghan history, Habibia Sorobi.

Segregating men and women in public is common in Afghanistan. During the Taliban's reign, strict and misguided interpretations of Islamic law (*shari'a*) and the Quran were implemented, many of which severely oppressed women. For example, young girls were prohibited from attending school and women were barred from the workplace. The burqa had to be worn by women in public—those caught wearing makeup or stylish clothes were beaten by the Taliban's religious police—and they were forbidden to leave the house without a close male relative escorting them.

At a typical rally, thousands of people line the streets; others hang out of their vehicles waving flags and banners. Even as a journalist I often can't get near the candidates and have to struggle to make my way through the crowds. Of course, there are press conferences, too, just as in North America. But it's better to be closer to the action.

All the candidates will talk to journalists, no problem. In many cases they are more willing to talk to journalists and to be photographed than politicians in North America.

Once, I got near a candidate just as he was finishing his speech. A group of photographers ran toward him as he jumped into his truck. Behind them was a huge crush of people closing in on the candidate, too, kicking up stormy clouds of dust in the process. I ran with them, trying to take a few frames as I went, but everybody was pretty much on top of me.

I ended up losing my driver and the car we'd come in. The only way back was to hitch a ride to Kabul.

CAMPAIGN RALLY IN ISTALIF VALLEY, NORTH OF KABUL

On a normal day, trying to get from point A to point B in Afghanistan can be challenging. On the day of a political rally, it's a hundred times worse! Today a number of other journalists and I made it to one by cramming into a pickup truck that was part of a candidate's convoy. Six or seven photographers sat in the truck bed and in the back seat, and a couple of reporters sat up front. It was tight.

A group of Afghan police officers led the way. Behind them came the candidate with his security. We were next, and behind us was another set of police officers. The drivers were all determined to get there. They wound through traffic without stopping for anybody, honking their horns, swerving in and out. The truck had no seatbelts, so I tied myself down with my scarf to avoid falling out when we flew over bumps in the unpaved roads. People waved madly at the convoy as we passed.

As usual, the crowd at the rally was huge. The cheering was deafening. And out of nowhere, a boxing match broke out. Only at an Afghan presidential rally!

We got lucky at this rally and were able to have lunch with the candidate and all the village elders. We sat away from the crowds in a beautiful garden filled with fruit trees. People brought us food—rice, bread, some vegetables, salad—and we sat for about an hour, eating and chatting. We didn't discuss

politics; we chatted about everyday stuff. The candidate told us a little bit about the area's history, how the Taliban had destroyed some of it.

What the candidates want for Afghanistan depends on which one you talk to, but while they might express it differently, in the end they all end up telling you the same thing. They want to put an end to corruption, to get the foreign troops out, to generate more jobs, and to have security handed over to the Afghans. The politicians, just as in North America, are looking out for the interests of the particular group they represent, and each group faces its own issues and has its own set of priorities. So while their specific visions for Afghanistan can be wildly different, they all claim that their priority is building a better future for their country.

Persian, Greek, Turkish, Mongol, and Mogul dynasties have all ruled the territory of Afghanistan at different times over a long period dating back 2,000 years. The modern state of Afghanistan began in the 18th century, when a young man named Ahmad Shah united various Pashtun tribes in the Hindu Kush Mountains and conquered the surrounding areas. The empire of Ahmad Shah became known as Afghanistan, or "land of the Afghans." Afghanistan remained under a Pashtun dynasty until 1973. The modern state of Afghanistan was born in 1919, following the Treaty of Rawalpindi, which granted the country independence from Great Britain and allowed Afghanistan to control its own foreign policy.

CAMPAIGN RALLY IN KABUL

At another campaign rally I went to, in Kabul, people raced to climb the light posts that circled the stadium. A helicopter flew overhead, dropping flyers. The politicians were treated like rock stars—the crowd went wild when one walked in. For a fleeting moment at least, it seemed the people believed in the candidate, daring to feel hopeful that his promises weren't empty.

I face a lot of challenges in crowds like that: pickpockets, the shoving and pushing, the struggle to get to where I need to be. Even when I am in the spot designated for media, still the crowd pushes forward, trying to get closer. It makes me feel very vulnerable. Ever present in the back of my mind is the thought that someone could sneak in explosives or that a suicide bomber could detonate himself, either near one of the candidates or in the crowd. I have to stay on my toes, scan the crowd, be aware of what's happening around me.

Of course, I can't really tell if someone is a bomber. Sometimes people spot them, but by then it's usually too late. Most of the time there's no warning. The explosion just happens.

KABUL

Today I was struck again by how reminders of war—past and present—are everywhere in Afghanistan. Inside the old blown-out, abandoned Russian building in this picture, the Afghans have set up rooms with punching bags, wrestling mats, and the like. It's barely lit, and on the crumbling walls are painted symbols depicting mines and rockets. I can't help but think of home, where I walk on the streets and see murals of trains or kids playing, or flowers. Here it's a whole other kind of graffiti.

Every day, families send their kids to this makeshift gym. And every day they walk by this wall—this is what they know. The symbols on it are from back in the time when the Soviet Union was occupying the country. Now it is a permanent reminder of war.

Do people even notice it any more? When I started photographing it, a young guy stood watching, his shadow thrown up on the wall. He looked as if he was trying to see in it what I saw. It's like living in Toronto or New York and seeing tourists take pictures of things you see every day. You are so used to it that you wouldn't think of taking its picture.

Imagine a young kid walking to school or going to get groceries, and every day he or she walks by painted symbols of rockets, mines, explosives, mortars—everything representing death. Maybe that young guy thought it was weird that I had even noticed it. I thought it weird that it had become so commonplace in his daily life that he didn't really see it anymore.

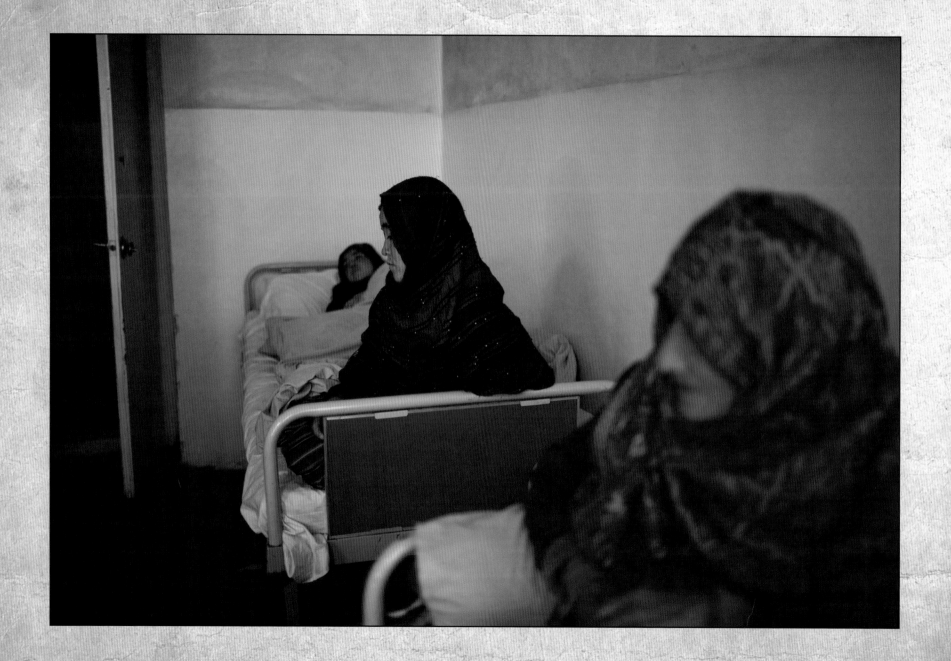

KABUL

I went to the drug and mental illness center today and asked for a tour, so that I would be able to take photographs. We went through the women's ward first. I don't know if anything could have prepared me for the things I saw there, and the stories I heard. I met women and young girls who had lost so much. One girl had suffered a breakdown after losing her young brother in a suicide bombing in Kabul; she had ended up in the ward with her mother. They allowed me to photograph them.

The women asked me to bring a copy of the photo back for them. I got it printed and brought it back the next day. They were surprised, and genuinely pleased.

"You brought it back!" the mother said to me. "We didn't know if we could trust you to."

I shrugged. "When I tell you I'm going to do something, I'm going to do it."

"Maybe it's just foreign men that keep their word," the woman replied.

I visited the men's ward, too. I met an Afghan soldier there in the drug rehabilitation center. He had been on the front lines and found himself turning to heroin and opium to deal with the stress. Soon he was addicted, and eventually he had a breakdown. This is very common— addiction is on the rise in Afghanistan, including among Afghan soldiers and police officers. It's a big problem.

This man's family is very supportive and helped him get into treatment. He's free to leave but he wants to be there. He'll get pretty much the kind of help he would in North America: medications, therapy, support. He's lucky: because he is a soldier, the government pays for his stay.

KABUL

Today I tagged along with an American doctor who was visiting some children's and military hospitals.

In Afghanistan, people pay for health care. Most can't afford any at all, so they just don't get treated. Unless they're seriously injured in a bombing, from driving over a mine, or anything else war-related, they generally don't see a doctor. They just find a way to live with the problem.

At one of our stops today, we met two Afghan soldiers injured in a suicide bombing. One had no idea where he was or what had happened; he didn't even know his own name. He had absolutely no memory of anything that had happened before he woke up in the hospital.

We also visited the International Community of the Red Cross and met a man waiting for a prosthetic leg. He was a goat- and sheep-herder; one day, while walking in the mountains outside Kabul, he'd stepped on a land mine and lost his leg. After he gets a prosthetic one, he'll go back to herding.

At the Red Cross center there are many, many like him: young kids, men, women. It's horrific to walk in and see all the war wounds. Most patients there are civilians, but the Red Cross will see Afghan soldiers, Taliban, and everybody else who comes in. They have no restrictions on who they will help.

Coming to these medical centers is the worst. Out in the field I'll see a few people who have been hurt, but when I'm in a hospital there are masses of them. When you see it in such a confined space, you can't ignore the extent of the injury, death, and trauma brought about by the conflict. It's devastating.

Walking into one of these places is like opening a portal to another dimension. They are so hard to photo-graph. I've watched people take their last breath and I've heard the cries of children, mothers, fathers, young men ... the screams and cries ...

This type of stuff happens every day in Afghanistan, and the medical centers are overwhelmed. I hope that one day this is no longer the norm, that these types of services won't have to exist for war victims. Maybe one day this will change in Afghanistan.

KABUL

I've been going to some refugee camps in Kabul. As difficult as they are to visit, I'm sure it's much more difficult to call them home. Many of the people there have come back from nearby Pakistan, where they fled because of the Taliban or the violence of the occupation. Others have escaped from fighting in the various provinces of Afghanistan. They've all come to Kabul with hopes for a better future, for work, for a school to send their kids to—but then they end up in these shacks, these makeshift shelters. Some are made out of just cloth and mud and sticks. The lucky refugees have tents.

Today I watched as the elders and children gathered for a doctor's visit. The doctor was explaining simple things to them, such as how to wash their hands properly and how to avoid eye infections. He's an American who visits all these camps alone. Everything he has—medicine, equipment,

first aid supplies—was donated, and he goes from camp to camp to talk to the elders and volunteer his services. They usually set up a little clinic in one of the huts, and people line up for consultations. For many, it's their first ever visit with a doctor.

Refugee camps are popping up all over Kabul and its outskirts. It's a terrible sight: children, adults, the elderly, all living in extreme poverty, without jobs, having lost family members in Taliban or coalition bombings. There is some order amid all the turmoil, though: as in any Afghan village, the elders are in charge. They do their best with what they have.

Some camps are massive, with thousands of people; some house maybe a dozen families. There are wells in the area, and every day people haul large plastic containers back and forth to get water. Areas are set aside to go to the bathroom, but a lot of the time people just squat in the ditches.

REFUGEES—During the conflict that raged in Afghanistan during the 1980s, more than five million Afghans were displaced, mostly to Pakistan, Iran, India, and the United Arab Emirates; another two million were displaced within their own country. The refugee crisis poses a major challenge to efforts to bring order to Afghanistan. Many Afghans have returned to a country full of corruption and have had to endure ongoing conflict, lack of basic services, and high unemployment.

At one of these camps I got a rare chance to photograph a woman. She was pleading with the volunteer doctor, asking for medicine for various problems she was having. His supply of medications was limited, and he didn't have enough to give her that day.

At first the woman didn't want to be photographed, but her husband, another refugee, told her it was okay. It's always difficult to take pictures of women, and I have to be careful. They've really been conditioned not to be photographed. Even young schoolgirls, who are allowed show their faces before they reach a certain age, hide behind their books as soon as I lift my camera. If I try to photograph women on the street, men often get upset.

Because it's so difficult for a man to photograph women in Afghanistan, I feel privileged when I am allowed to. The women want their stories told, too. If they know they won't be punished—by their husband or another man or a family member—they want me to take their picture; they want people to know what they're going through.

It's hard to imagine what will happen to the people in these camps. Some will be lucky enough to find jobs and maybe housing somewhere else, but most will stay for years. I've seen photographs taken almost twenty years ago in the same areas. Not much has changed.

KABUL

Today I went shopping at one of the Western-style grocery stores that have popped up here, where I can get everything that I'm used to from back home. It's all more expensive, of course, and targeted to foreigners and the wealthy. You'll never find your average Afghan shopping in one. I do feel conflicted about that: I don't like going where most locals can't afford to shop.

Outside, a war widow was begging for money. Afghanistan has a lot of war widows—many men have died fighting over the years. Widows and orphans will often either try washing windows or beg for money outside these stores. I haven't seen many men doing the same.

There isn't much in Afghanistan for these

Women were not always as oppressed as they were during the Taliban era. In 1977 women held 15 percent of Afghanistan's highest legislative positions, and prior to the Taliban's ascent to power, 70 percent of Afghan schoolteachers, 50 percent of government employees, and 40 percent of doctors in Kabul were women. Women continue to struggle to find an acceptable place in society—between modernity and tradition—in Afghanistan.

women. Some small charities help out, but money is scarce. Women who are left without husbands or fathers are better off if they have a son who can get work and take care of the family. If the women have no one, they might get lucky and find a job. But not many jobs are available to them, and most of these women don't have an education—without that, their options are even slimmer.

These women are hard to miss in their bright blue burqas, but people will walk by them as if they're not even there. In Afghanistan, women are often sold off, beaten down, or killed. They're seen more as the property of men than as their equals.

A CHILDREN'S HOSPITAL IN KABUL

Today I stopped at a children's hospital in Kabul with another foreign volunteer doctor. Even before we got inside, the doctor went to work, helping a father who was standing at the doors holding his child. The man had been waiting, hoping for help. His child was totally dehydrated; the helplessness this man felt was written starkly across his face.

The doctor gave the child water and his eyes opened. Something as simple as water had already started to make him feel better.

This doctor invited me along on his rounds today because he wanted me to see how bad the situation is in some of these hospitals. He had been to this hospital many times, and that helped us get access. We walked along corridors that were without electricity. Flies buzzed incessantly, and the rotten stench of dirty sheets stained with urine and feces filled the air. There was no air conditioning and it was stifling. I saw no medical supplies, there wasn't proper ventilation, every room was over-crowded ... I could go on and on.

The hospital was filled with young children who were ill, malnourished, dehydrated, waiting to be treated. Some had been left, abandoned by their parents; others were there with their mothers only. This mother with her dying baby son caught my eye.

Sitting there, draped in black, she reminded me of an angel of death, waiting for this young child to go so she could take his soul. There is a strange calmness in the way the mothers wait so quietly and patiently.

The doctor, I think, was living with post-traumatic stress disorder. We had stayed at the same hotel, and he sometimes came out of his room, confused, asking me, "Those guys that are looking for me, are they gone?" At times, maybe after a long day, he wouldn't know where he was, what we had done earlier, or what we had talked about.

He travels to many conflict zones, not just Afghanistan: he's been to Georgia and Iraq and places that have had tsunamis or earthquakes. He's always one of the first responders. Whether it's finding medicine for my tooth infection, helping an elder in a refugee camp, or picking up bodies after a tsunami, he'll be there. He's a good man; he's willing to help people no matter what, but it comes at a great cost to him psychologically.

I really admire people who do this sort of work, either at home or abroad. I often stop and think how amazing it is what they—doctors, nurses, paramedics, firefighters—do for us, and the types of situations they put themselves in to help others. I thank them as often as I can.

KABUL

COMBAT MEDICAL KIT

This morning I was in my hotel room in downtown Kabul, getting ready for the day, when I heard a thump. Actually, it wasn't even that I heard it. I felt it, right in my gut. The windows in the hotel shook. A bomb had exploded close by.

I poked my head out the door at the same time as another photographer. Both of us ran up to the roof to look for the cloud of smoke that would tell us what direction to head in. We found it, looked at each other, and knew: okay, we're ready to go.

Downstairs, another journalist joined us as we hailed a taxi. We didn't have an interpreter, so we just flashed a bunch of money, pointed to the smoke, and said, "Get us to the bombing."

The cabbie got us to the point where the road was blocked. We jumped out and ran down the street. After these bombings, people are trying to get away, running, scattering—and there we were, three guys with cameras, going straight toward it.

We neared the bombing site, which was at the American embassy and the International Security Assistance Force headquarters across the street. I saw victims being treated, extra Afghan soldiers arriving on the scene to help, and even staff from the National Department of Security—basically Afghanistan's CIA. The Afghan police officers started becoming very hostile toward the journalists, raising their weapons, threatening us, trying to move us out of the danger zone in case there was a second bomb. Often there is.

We knew we weren't going to get any closer to the scene. I turned to another photographer and said, "It's not really about the scene anymore. It's about the victims, the civilians. Let's head over to the hospital."

The hospital was blocked off. Crowds of people were already sitting outside, and more were gathering. Some people were crying, some were injured. We couldn't tell if they were victims of the bombing, family members, or people who were ill and just trying to see a doctor. It was chaotic, to say the least.

The Afghan police officer outside the hospital door was very, very agitated. He didn't want to let us in.

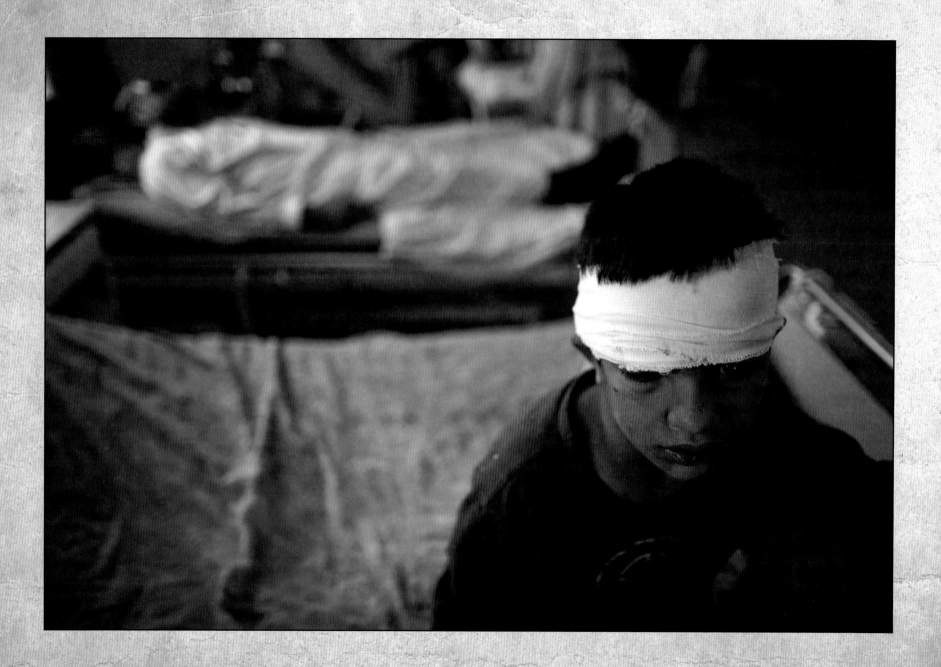

My friend spoke a little bit of Dari, and that got us past the officer and into the hospital to speak to the director.

We explained to the director why we were there and why it was important to see the victims, to talk to them and photograph them; that we wanted to get these pictures out to the world because this was what the conflict was about—these were the people most affected by it.

He agreed to let us through. The ward was filled with boys and men ranging in age from about twelve to maybe their mid-fifties. I scoured the room, as I always do, and tried to get permission to take photographs. In these situations it's not easy. It's one thing for a person to allow you into his everyday life, but it's another thing for him to consent to being photographed after he has survived something like this.

The twelve-year-old boy in this photograph was sitting on the edge of a bed. I gestured with my camera and he nodded. The doctor told me the boy had just been passing by when the suicide bomber detonated a vehicle, killing many and injuring more. Most of them were civilian bystanders.

I can't imagine that being my reality: waking up in the morning to go to the store, go for a walk, go get the mail, and a bomb going off. How do parents raise kids in a situation like that? How does a kid, an innocent human being, cope with this? How do they find the inner strength to go on? It takes amazing courage. I can't imagine seeing my little brother, my cousin, my son like this.

PUL-I-CHARKHI PRISON, EAST OF KABUL

I visited Pul-i-Charkhi Prison today with another photographer and a driver/interpreter. I got chills as we approached; it was not like the well-maintained buildings sitting on perfectly manicured grounds that we call jails in North America. The thick bars in the windows were rusted out and filthy; the walls of the building were full of bullet holes from years of fighting. It was not a place where anyone would want to live.

Inside, we were granted permission to speak to some Taliban and other insurgents. The man in this picture, Habad, was a would-be suicide bomber.

It took a little while to get him to open up to us. At first he was reluctant to talk. He was very nervous, so we explained why we were there and what we were doing—that we were specifically looking for Taliban and insurgents to speak to. We wanted his side of the story.

I rarely have a chance to talk to insurgents and ask them what I want to know: Why do they believe what they believe? Why are they fighting? What are they fighting for? How do they look at Westerners? How do they see this conflict that has plagued their country for years? I felt grateful to have the opportunity and I wanted Habad to feel comfortable enough to share his story.

He said he'd speak to us only if the guard would leave. The rules of conduct are different from those in North American prisons, and for some reason the guard agreed. Who knows, maybe he was

Jihad is a complicated concept, and even many Muslims disagree about its precise definition. To non-Muslims it has become synonymous with "holy war," but its true meaning is more complex and involves Muslims' struggle to preserve their faith. Its literal translation is "to strive" or "to struggle." Although most Muslims see this as an internal struggle, extremists have used it as an excuse to fight wars against perceived oppressors. The term *jihad* became a powerful mobilization tool during the Soviet invasion and occupation of Afghanistan in the 1980s; it united many Afghans to fight against the Communist government forces and their Soviet supporters. These Afghan resistance fighters called themselves mujahideen—"holy warriors"—and they led a campaign of guerrilla warfare that lasted almost twelve years. Today the term *jihad* remains a rallying call for Islamic fundamentalist groups and terrorist organizations to mobilize their followers into military action against perceived domestic or international threats.

intimidated by my interpreter, who was a pretty big guy.

Habad started telling us about how he had been recruited in Pakistan. He had met an old friend who told him about the Taliban and the fight in Afghanistan. He decided to learn more about it.

When he met with the insurgents, they showed him videos of NATO bombings in Afghanistan. They told him that coalition forces were killing innocent Afghans and that Muslims were being killed without cause. Habad decided he would take part himself and do something about it.

Habad told me that the videos he was shown were what had driven him to find the strength within himself to take part in the jihad—the holy war. He prepared himself in Pakistan, along with other bombers; there are crews who train suicide bombers in groups. After his training, Habad loaded a car with explosives, drove over the border to Afghanistan, into Paktika province, and showed up at the base where he was supposed to blow himself up.

But as he sat there watching the base, all he saw were Afghan police officers and Afghan army soldiers, not foreigners. "When I arrived and saw no Americans, I could not bring myself to kill my Muslim brothers," he told me. He decided not to detonate the bomb and turned himself in instead.

Since then he's been in Pul-i-Charkhi Prison, awaiting trial. He didn't really want to be photographed—he is ashamed of himself and didn't want to be identified—so he covered his face while I took his picture.

I have video and pictures of suicide bombers preparing to blow themselves up, and they're smiling as they're about to press the detonator. How do the Taliban convince people to kill themselves? It's impossible to imagine the motivation behind it, unless you can understand getting to a point where you are willing to die for a cause.

What's really despicable is that they sometimes use kids as suicide bombers. Insurgents will strap bombs to children and make them run out in front of a convoy. The children often don't fully understand what's happening, so there is always someone with a remote nearby who triggers the blast.

I met with three men in that prison. All admitted to being with the Taliban or being associated with them in one way or another. I was surprised, and grateful, that they told me their stories—me, a foreigner, their perceived enemy, the kind of person they had set out to kill. We sat down face to face and had an honest conversation. I have to respect that.

KABUL

Right at sunrise, throughout the streets of Kabul, the butchers hang out their wares in preparation for a day of selling. The animals are killed either the night before or early that morning. People from other parts of the city come to buy these big slabs of meat for resale.

Everything is done outside—it's totally differently from North American practice. There are no fridges. Flies and all sorts of insects crawl over the meat as it's being prepared. It's not unusual to get sick from eating it.

From sunrise to sunset, Afghanistan is a busy place. But once the sun goes down, the streets are deserted, the stores are closed, and everybody goes home.

Everyone, it seems, except workers at the brick factory. Smoke belches from the chimneys at the brick factory in Kabul twenty-four hours a day. The place in this photo produces 21,000 bricks per day, or 630,000 bricks per month. It employs between 80 and 100 workers, including both adult and child laborers, and sometimes whole families.

All this work is done outside, too. It's a hot and dangerous job: it's easy to get burned and easy to fall into the ovens—holes in the ground about the size of a large pizza—that are used to heat the bricks. The children carry bricks, mix some of the materials together, haul water—anything that's asked of them. Child labor is a problem in Afghanistan. At the market, for example, anyone can buy weapons from a twelve-year-old kid. If labor laws exist, they're not enforced. Any job that a man does, a child could do. You see it every day.

I spent a couple of hours at the brick factory, photographing these guys at work. They were very friendly. At break time they set a pot of chai on the forge to boil. That was pretty innovative.

ROQIA CENTER FOR WOMEN'S RIGHTS, STUDIES AND EDUCATION, KABUL

Nasrine Gross, an Afghan woman who lives in America now, regularly returns to Kabul. She comes back to teach classes in basic skills such as reading and writing and in women's rights, to both men and women. She invited me to attend one.

Nasrine runs these classes once a week through the Roqia Center for Women's Rights. The center is an organization meant to be a vehicle for change, but it has no office or designated meeting space. So the teacher and her pupils meet in different students' homes, in their spare rooms, or in whatever space they can find. It's safer to run the classes this way, going from place to place. There are people who would get upset about these kinds of things being taught in their neighborhood. Women do attend alone sometimes, but most of them are with their husbands.

When I first walked in, it was very difficult to get a photograph. I arrived before Nasrine, and when her students saw me, the women scrambled to cover up. The men, too, looked very upset by my being there.

As soon as Nasrine walked in, she noticed the difference my presence had made. "This is why these classes are happening! Do not cover your faces," she told the women, raising her voice. Then, to the men: "You have to be okay with allowing another man to see your women, to photograph your women." It was really good to see a woman stand up for other women and for what she believes in. She lectured them a while longer, and finally they opened up and let me take some pictures.

Nasrine walks around the streets of Kabul without covering up—not her face, her hair, or anything. It's safer to do this in Kabul than in rural Afghanistan, but it's still risky.

As we were leaving today's class, she was the only woman who wasn't covered. A group of men nearby made their discontent apparent. You could sense the disrespect they felt, even from a distance. If we had stuck around longer, there would have been a confrontation; to avoid any trouble we just got in the cars and left.

Nasrine is used to all of this now. Her house has been trashed by people opposed to what she does; her life has been threatened. But she doesn't let that stop her, She often sleeps in a different place every night, moving from friend's place to friend's place or hotel to hotel, and she keeps on teaching.

She's a very brave woman.

KABUL

During the holy month of Ramadan, Muslims restrict their eating and drinking during the day, and then families break the fast after sunset. Tonight, my last night in Afghanistan, my driver and I passed a family breaking the fast as is customary. They had spread their meal on a blanket laid out on the sidewalk. They didn't mind me hanging around, so I knelt down closer to take a photograph. I really like the light just after sunset.
It was a nice moment.

Ramadan, which occurs in the sacred ninth month of the Islamic lunar calendar, is when the Prophet Muhammad received the first revelation of the Quran. Muslims are required to fast from dawn till sunset during Ramadan. Healthy Muslim adults must not eat or drink, chew gum, use tobacco, or have intercourse during this time. They are also prohibited from gossiping, telling lies, or making unkind remarks to others. During this period, Muslims strive for purity in their thoughts and actions, seek forgiveness for past transgressions, and ask for guidance in the future.

Muslims believe that observing Ramadan helps to bring them closer to God, by teaching patience, humility, and self-restraint. The final ten days of Ramadan are especially holy, a time when angels are thought to descend during the night to bless mankind. Ramadan concludes with Eid al-Fitr, the feast of breaking the fast. This is one of two great Muslim holidays, and Muslims observe the celebration by feasting, giving alms, and attending religious services.

Afghan food is delicious: the varieties of bread, the different rice, the salads. The Afghans' diet is made up mostly of potatoes, vegetables, and meat. The dishes are usually chunky, like a stew, and people eat the food with rice or bread—naan. They use plates, but their hands are their utensils. Most of the time a family shares a plate. You rip off a piece of bread and grab the food with it. Sometimes you sit on chairs around a regular table, but it's more common to sit on the ground on a plastic sheet or at a very low table.

One of my favorite foods is bolani. It's a deep-fried pancake with diced green onions and potatoes mashed together, and it's made for you right on the street. In Afghan currency it's 10 afs—the equivalent of 18 or 20 cents—for one. Bolani is a real comfort food. I can taste it now. I'll miss it when I'm gone, and I wonder if—when—I'll be back to eat it again.

AFTERWORD

I did go back to Afghanistan again; in fact, I went back to embed with the same American troops I had been with on my first visit. But something was different, and I realized that it was me. I still had a connection to the guys, we were still friendly, but now I had seen the other side of things.

When I first went to Afghanistan and embedded with these guys, as much as I thought otherwise, I really knew nothing about the people or the culture of the country. But after living there on my own and spending more time exploring and learning about the place, I grew closer to the Afghans I met. I felt more a part of their community, more aware of their culture. I wanted people outside of Afghanistan to look at my photos and feel that way, too—for them to understand that there's so much more than a war going on there.

On this visit I became uncomfortable with the military side of things, so I ended up leaving the embed early. I went back to documenting civilian life, of the Hazara people in particular. They are an ethnic group originally from Mongolia who have long been oppressed by the Taliban. Their story is one of struggle, but also of hope; it spoke to me more than what was going on with the military occupation.

Over the years, with everything I've experienced and witnessed there, I'd be lying if I said I didn't have a bit of a love/hate relationship with Afghanistan. But despite a lot of the ugliness that goes on there, the country has an undeniable underlying beauty. You can see it in the sprawling Panjshir landscape, the openness of Afghan hospitality, and especially in the clear will of the people to survive. In spite of everything, Afghans stay strong and hopeful. And as long as they have stories they want to tell, I'll keep going back.

THE ETHNIC GROUPS OF AFGHANISTAN

PASHTUNS

The largest ethnic group in Afghanistan, comprising around 42 percent of the population, is the Pashtuns. This cultural group has retained a tribal identity, with a social structure of tribal leader, elders (*spin giri*), and wealthy landowners (*khans*) who shape local communities by maintaining order and upholding a code of honor (*pashtunwali*). Pashtuns are well known for their strong desire for independence, pride, and dignity. They were the first ethnic group to unify the country, by establishing the independent kingdom of Afghanistan in 1747.

TAJIKS

Tajiks make up around 27 percent of the Afghan population. Known as *farsiwans*, or "Persian-speakers," Tajiks can usually be found in the plains areas of Herat (on Afghanistan's border with Iran), the central highlands near Bamyian, and around Kabul, where they engage in trading, skilled craft-making, and farming. In the mountainous areas of northeastern Afghanistan, they are village-dwelling farmers. Unlike other ethnic groups in Afghanistan, it is Tajik landowners, not tribal leaders, who have emerged as important village leaders.

UZBEKS

Uzbeks (around 9 percent of the Afghan population) are a Sunni Turkish-speaking group descended from nomadic tribal confederations from central Asia. Uzbeks in Afghanistan arrived sometime during the sixteenth century in a series of conquering waves, but most later settled in the northwest and became farmers.

HAZARAS

Making up around 9 percent of Afghanistan's population, Hazaras are Shi'a Muslims who operate small farms and produce and care for domestic animals. They speak a dialect of Persian but are thought to descend from the Mongol armies that once conquered Iran. They had their own independent mountain state (Hazarajat) until the Afghan king Abul Rahman conquered it, forcing many Hazara into slavery. Modern Pashtun Taliban forces brutalized the Hazara once more; many Hazara in northern Afghanistan allied themselves with Uzbek militias who battled against Taliban forces between 1996 and 2001.

ACKNOWLEDGMENTS

Life in Afghanistan is not easy for many and it wasn't easy for me. Thank-you can't describe the appreciation I feel for all the people who supported me along the way and still do today. My family, friends, colleagues, and strangers all played a big role in the success of delivering messages from Afghanistan. Most of all the people in my images are the ones who deserve the credit. I am their messenger, but they are the ones with the message. My job would not be possible without the people who put themselves in harm's way just as I did to show the world both the humanity and horror of the war. My Afghan friends and strangers who don't get to escape this reality—you are in my thoughts every day.

Tashakur, Manana, thank-you.

Special thanks to 1st Lt. Nick A. Dewhirst, CPL. Peter Courcy, PVT. Toby Phillips, SGT. Barbara Ospina, Samsoor Momand, the staff at Hotel Mustafa, Carmine Marinelli, Jayson Taylor, and my trusty sidekick, friend, and driver, Barialie Abdul Ali.

There are still way too many folks to list, including all the staff at Annick Press and Sharon McKay for believing in this work. And I can't forget all my friends who let me couch surf on my trips back to Canada; my door is always open to you.

ABOUT RAFAL GERSZAK

Born in Poland, Rafal Gerszak was forced with his family to flee their home during the Soviet era and live for some time in a West German refugee camp. After immigrating to Canada in 1990, he began to identify with socially displaced groups and spent time documenting drug culture in Vancouver, Canada's, downtown eastside before moving to Afghanistan.

A graduate of the Photography Program at Langara College in Vancouver, Rafal specializes in long-term documentary projects focusing on communities and people in the under-class of Canadian society, and on the conflict in Afghanistan. His work has been exhibited internationally including at The New York Photo Festival and Noorderlicht Photofestival in the Netherlands. His photographs have been published in newspapers and magazines worldwide.

His documentary work and short films from Afghanistan and Canada have been recognized by The National Press Photographers Association and News Photographers Association of Canada. In 2010, he was selected as one of the winners of Flash Forward, The Magenta Foundation's international competition for emerging photographers.

A sincere thank-you to expert consultant Matthew C. DuPee, senior research associate with the Program for Culture and Conflict Studies, Naval Postgraduate School, for his time and efforts.

Designed by Sheryl Shapiro

Annick Press Ltd.

We acknowledge the support of the Canada Council for the Arts, the Ontario Arts Council, and the Government of Canada through the Canada Book Fund (CBF) for our publishing activities.

ONTARIO ARTS COUNCIL
CONSEIL DES ARTS DE L'ONTARIO

Images ©Rafal Gerszak with the following exceptions: **front cover, 1: scrap paper,** ©Les Cunliffe; **front and back cover and throughout book, except where specified: paper background,** ©Jakub Krechowicz; **2: map,** ©Beholderey; **7, 23, 27, 35, 51, 70: maps,** ©Indos82; **11, 19, 22, 61: note paper,** ©Raja Rc; **17, 33, 59, 65, 67, 75, 76, 79, 97, 110, 119: scrap paper,** ©Robyn Mackenzie; **36, 95, back cover: scrap paper,** ©Toh Eng Chai; **73: darker paper in foreground,** ©Batman2000; **125: four papers in foreground,** ©Picsfive; all ©Dreamstime.com; **1: foreground photograph; 13: foreground photograph; 40: foreground photograph; 50: inside photograph; 72: foreground photograph,** ©Farhad Naser; **127: foreground photograph,** ©P. J. Tobia.

Cataloging in Publication

Gerszak, Rafal
    Beyond bullets : a photo journal of Afghanistan / by Rafal Gerszak ; with Dawn Hunter ; photographs by Rafal Gerszak.

ISBN 978-1-55451-293-5

    1. Afghanistan—Juvenile literature. 2. Afghanistan—Social conditions—Juvenile literature. 3. Afghanistan—Pictorial works—Juvenile literature. I. Hunter, Dawn II. Title.

DS352.G47 2011   j958.104'70222   C2011-902432-2

Distributed in Canada by:
Firefly Books Ltd.
66 Leek Crescent
Richmond Hill, ON
L4B 1H1

Published in the U.S.A. by Annick Press (U.S.) Ltd.
Distributed in the U.S.A. by:
Firefly Books (U.S.) Inc.
P.O. Box 1338
Ellicott Station
Buffalo, NY 14205

Printed in China

Visit us at: www.annickpress.com
Visit Rafal Gerszak at: www.gerszak.com

For the people I love and for those I have lost
—D. H.